Novels for Students, Volume 10

Staff

Series Editors: Michael L. LaBlanc and Ira Mark Milne.

Contributing Editors: Elizabeth Bellalouna, Elizabeth Bodenmiller, Reginald Carlton, Anne Marie Hacht, Polly Rapp, Jennifer Smith.

Research: Victoria B. Cariappa, *Research Team Manager*. Maureen Eremic, Barb McNeil, Cheryl Warnock, *Research Specialists*. Andy Malonis, *Technical Training Specialist*. Barbara Leevy, Tamara Nott, Tracie A. Richardson, Robert Whaley, *Research Associates*. Scott Floyd, Nicodemus Ford, Sarah Genik, Timothy Lehnerer, *Research Assistants*.

Permissions: Maria Franklin, *Permissions Manager*. Margaret A. Chamberlain, Edna Hedblad, *Permissions Specialists*. Erin Bealmear, Shalice Shah-Caldwell, Sarah Tomasek, *Permissions*

Associates. Debra Freitas, Julie Juengling, Mark Plaza, *Permissions Assistants.*

Manufacturing: Mary Beth Trimper, *Manager, Composition and Electronic Prepress.* Evi Seoud, *Assistant Manager, Composition Purchasing and Electronic Prepress.* Stacy Melson, *Buyer.*

Imaging and Multimedia Content Team: Randy Bassett, *Image Database Supervisor.* Robert Duncan, Dan Newell, *Imaging Specialists.* Pamela A. Reed, *Imaging Coordinator.* Dean Dauphinais, Robyn V. Young, *Senior Image Editors.* Kelly A. Quin, *Image Editor.*

Product Design Team: Kenn Zorn, *Product Design Manager.* Pamela A. E. Galbreath, *Senior Art Director.* Michael Logusz, *Graphic Artist.*

Copyright Notice

Since this page cannot legibly accommodate all copyright notices, the acknowledgments constitute an extension of the copyright notice.

While every effort has been made to secure permission to reprint material and to ensure the reliability of the information presented in this publication, Gale Research neither guarantees the accuracy of the data contained herein nor assumes any responsibility for errors, omissions, or discrepancies. Gale accepts no payment for listing; and inclusion in the publication of any organization, agency, institution, publication, service, or individual does not imply endorsement of the editors or publisher. Errors brought to the attention of the publisher and verified to the satisfaction of the publisher will be corrected in future editions.

This publication is a creative work fully protected by all applicable copyright laws, as well as by misappropriation, trade secret, unfair competition, and other applicable laws. The authors and editors of this work have added value to the underlying factual material herein through one or more of the following: unique and original selection, coordination, expression, arrangement, and classification of the information. All rights to this publication will be vigorously defended.

Copyright © 2001
Gale Group
27500 Drake Rd.
Farmington Hills, MI 48331-3535

All rights reserved including the right of reproduction in whole or in part in any form.

ISBN 0-7876-3829-3
ISSN 1094-3552

Printed in the United States of America.
10 9 8 7 6 5 4 3 2 1

Howards End

E. M. Forster 1910

Introduction

When *Howards End* was published in 1910, critics generally agreed it surpassed E. M. Forster's earlier novels. Forster had arrived as an important author, and the public and critics eagerly anticipated his next novel. But fourteen years would elapse before the publication of *A Passage to India*, which would also be the last novel published during his lifetime. Forster's novels are all considered classics, with *Howards End* and *A Passage to India* regarded as his best works. Like all of Forster's early novels, *Howards End* concerns itself with Edwardian society. As a member of the upper-middle class,

Forster had keen insight into its attitudes and social mores, which he expertly rendered in *Howards End*. His humanistic values and interest in personal relationships inform all of his novels, and are revealed in the major themes of *Howards End:* connection between the inner and outer life and between people, the future of England, and class conflicts. *Howards End* has been called a parable; indeed, its symbolism reaches almost mythic proportions at various points in the novel. Although elements of the plot construction have been problematic for some critics, opinion of his character creation and development is almost unanimously given the highest praise. With Margaret Schlegel, Henry Wilcox, Helen Schlegel, Leonard Bast, and Forster created some of the most unforgettable and complex characters in English literature.

Author Biography

Edward Morgan Forster was born on January 1, 1879, in Coventry, England. His father died when he was only a year and a half old, leaving him to the care of his mother and a devoted circle of female relatives. He and his mother lived at Rooksnest, their beloved country house near Stevenage in Hertfordshire. After a rather unhappy adolescence as a student at Tonbridge School, Forster enrolled at Cambridge University, where he flourished.

At Cambridge the emphasis was on liberal arts and individual expression; Forster found freedom to pursue both intellectual development and personal relationships. It was here that he began developing many of the humanistic ideas and values that would come to dominate his literary works. He became a member of the Cambridge Apostles, an intellectual discussion group. Many Apostles were later active in the Bloomsbury Group, which began informal salons in London about 1905. Several in the Bloomsbury circle later became famous: Lytton Strachey as a critic, biographer, and historian; Leonard Woolf as political activist and theorist and man of letters; John Maynard Keynes as a political and economic theorist; Roger Fry and Clive Bell as art critics; Grant and Vanessa Bell as painters; and Virginia Woolf and Forster as novelists. The Bloomsbury Group was influenced by Cambridge philosophers, especially G. E. Moore, who believed in the value of social interaction and cultural stimuli, and possessed a passion for the truth and a skepticism toward moral tradition.

After Forster graduated from Cambridge in 1901, he traveled abroad for a year. Between 1902 and 1910, he wrote four novels: *Where Angels Fear To Tread* (1905), *A Room with a View* (1908), *The Longest Journey* (1907), and *Howards End* (1910). With *Howards End*, Forster achieved status as a major writer, receiving high critical praise. Forster's novels were recognized for their precise character portrayal, their concern with the complexities of human nature, and their detailed, comical descriptions of Edwardian society. His next novel, *A Passage to India*, did not appear until 1924, and was the last novel published during his lifetime. A posthumously published novel, *Maurice*, tells the story of a young man's growing awareness of his homosexuality and is based on Forster's own experiences. The publication of *A Passage to India* firmly established Forster's reputation as a master novelist. Drawn from Forster's experiences in India during visits there in 1912 and 1921, *A Passage to India* portrays the social and political realities of colonial India.

For the rest of his career, Forster focused on writing short stories, essays, biographies, and travel books. He also became quite politically active, and wrote essays in which he spoke out against many of the political and social ills of his time. In the mid-1940s he was offered a resident fellowship at Cambridge University, which he enthusiastically accepted. He became one of the most celebrated figures at the university, and remained active in university life and continued to write and publish well into the early 1960s. He died on June 7, 1970, in Coventry at the home of friends.

Plot Summary

Howards End begins with Helen Schlegel's brief affair with Paul Wilcox. In its wake, Helen's Aunt Juley travels to Howards End, the Wilcox home, to discuss the relationship with the Wilcoxes, not knowing that it has already ended. The Wilcoxes react with horror to news of the affair, believing, unlike the Schlegels, that Paul must make his fortune before he marries.

Helen, her romance with Paul and the rest of the Wilcox family over, returns to the Schlegel house, Wickham Place, and she and her sister Margaret resume their old life together. They attend a concert of Beethoven with other family members, and Helen accidentally walks off with the umbrella of Leonard Bast, a poor clerk teetering on the edge of respectability. After accompanying Margaret to Wickham Place to retrieve his umbrella, Leonard accepts her card, and returns to his own shabby flat, where he lives with Jacky, a woman much older than he.

The Schlegels learn that the Wilcoxes are taking a flat across the street from Wickham Place, and Ruth Wilcox soon calls on Margaret. Margaret writes a rude note suggesting that they should not meet because of the possibility of an encounter between Helen and Paul, and Mrs. Wilcox replies to her that they should meet, because there is no possibility of an encounter between the two former lovers. The two women strike up a friendship, in spite of Mrs. Wilcox's discomfort in Margaret's world. Mrs. Wilcox feels that Margaret understands her attachment to Howards End, and after a day of shopping together, she impulsively proposes they go there. Margaret wavers at first, but they leave for the train station, where they meet Henry and Evie Wilcox, Mrs. Wilcox's husband and daughter. Mrs. Wilcox is spirited off by her family, and Margaret's visit is postponed. Soon after, Mrs. Wilcox dies.

The Wilcoxes are alarmed to discover that Mrs. Wilcox has left a note leaving Howards End to Margaret. They decide to burn the note, and not speak of it to Margaret.

Two years pass. The Schlegels are about to lose their house at Wickham Place, which will be destroyed so that flats may be built there. Leonard Bast's wife, Jacky, comes round to the house looking for him. Leonard has disappeared for an evening, and Jacky thinks he is with the Schlegels. The next day, Bast appears at Wickham Place, explaining that he has taken an all-night walk outside of London. When he notes that the dawn was gray and not at all romantic, the Schlegels are charmed by him. When they mention Bast to Henry Wilcox, he tells them Bast's company is in danger of going under, and they resolve to warn Bast of this eventuality. They invite Bast to tea, and he is suspicious of their desire to talk business when he wants to talk poetry. The tea is interrupted when Evie and Henry Wilcox arrive at the house, and as Bast is leaving, he tells the Schlegels he will not call again. Mr. Wilcox thinks that Margaret is attracted to Leonard Bast, and feels an attraction for her as a result. Soon after, at a lunch with Evie, Mr. Wilcox offers to lease the Wilcoxes' Ducie Street flat to the Schlegels. While Margaret tours the flat, Mr. Wilcox asks her to marry him, and she accepts.

Margaret wants to live at Howards End, but her fiancé is against it. Meanwhile, Helen has had a letter from Leonard Bast, who is leaving his company for another post at lower pay. When Margaret mentions this to Henry, he says that in fact Bast's company is a very stable firm. Though the Schlegels blame Henry for Bast's predicament, he shrugs off their criticism.

Margaret and Henry make a trip to Howards End, where she is frightened by Miss Avery, who mistakes her for Ruth Wilcox. Margaret loves the house, but believes that she and Henry will live at Oniton, where they attend Evie's wedding to Percy Cahill. Helen, who has refused to attend the wedding, arrives there unexpectedly with Leonard and Jacky Bast, saying that she has found them starving. Margaret is planning to ask Henry to give Bast a place in his company, but before she can do so, Jacky recognizes Henry as her former lover. Helen takes the Basts to a hotel, where she and Leonard have an intimate conversation. Margaret, who believes Henry's unfaithfulness is the late Mrs. Wilcox's tragedy rather than hers, refuses Henry's offer to release her from their engagement, and they reconcile. Before Margaret can speak with any of them, Helen and the Basts leave their hotel.

Before she goes to Germany, Helen attempts to give the Basts a substantial monetary gift, but they refuse. They are soon evicted and forced to rely on handouts from Leonard's family. Wickham Place is destroyed to make way for flats, and Margaret and Henry marry. With the family scattered, the Schlegels' furniture is stored at Howards End. When Margaret hears that Miss Avery has unpacked the Schlegels' things, she goes to Howards End. She is amazed to see how well her furniture fits in the house, but is soon called away to Swanage when she gets news of her aunt's illness. Margaret and her brother Tibby contact Helen, who has been in Germany for eight months, to tell her Juley is gravely ill, and Helen agrees to come to Swanage. When Helen hears that Juley has recovered, she refuses to see her family, but will get some books from Howards End. Believing her sister to be unwell, Margaret reluctantly agrees to Henry's plan to surprise Helen at Howards End.

As the plan is carried out, Margaret realizes that "[t]he pack was turning on Helen, to deny her human rights," and it seems to Margaret "that all Schlegels were threatened with her." When she sees her sister, who is pregnant with Leonard Bast's child, she pushes her into Howards End, and bids her husband and the doctor to leave them. Helen, on seeing their furniture and other things, asks to spend the night in Howards End. When Margaret asks Henry if they may stay at Howards End, he refuses on the grounds that it would be immoral. Margaret is disgusted by his hypocrisy and she defies his wishes, spending a peaceful night at Howards End with her sister.

Leonard Bast has been looking for Margaret, and Tibby tells him she is at Howards End. As Leonard approaches the house, he is filled with happiness, but when he enters the house, Charles strikes him, and he dies. In the wake of Bast's death and her own quarrel with him, Margaret tells Henry she will go to Germany with Helen. But Henry is broken by the certainty of Charles's conviction for manslaughter, and Margaret takes him to recover at Howards End. In the final scene of the novel, fourteen months have passed, and Helen, her child by Leonard Bast, Margaret, and Henry have become a loving family. In the presence of his children, Henry deeds Howards End to Margaret, who will leave it to her sister's son. When Dolly remarks that Margaret has gotten Howards End after all, Margaret realizes that she has conquered the Wilcoxes without even trying.

Characters

Miss Avery

Miss Avery is Ruth Wilcox's old friend and the caretaker of Howards End. She unpacks and arranges the Schlegels' furniture in Howards End, even though it is only supposed to be stored there.

Jacky Bast

Jacky is Leonard's dull, uneducated wife who was once Henry Wilcox's mistress.

Leonard Bast

Leonard is the lowly clerk who wishes to educate himself by reading books and attending concerts. "Such a muddle of a man, and yet so worth pulling though," says Helen Schlegel. He is described as being on the "abyss" of poverty, and is very self-conscious about his position in society. Suspicious of the rich, he will not be patronized by them, which is part of the reason he refuses Helen's offer of money. His two unfortunate mistakes are leaving his job on the advice of the Schlegel sisters (and Henry Wilcox), and becoming involved with Helen. The scene in which he dies, which includes a dramatic fall into a bookcase that showers him with books, has been criticized for its heavy-handed symbolism.

Frieda Mosebach

Frieda Mosebach is the Schlegels' German cousin, who attends the performance of Beethoven's Fifth Symphony with them.

Juley Munt

Juley Munt is the Schlegels' beloved but interfering aunt, whose famously comic scene in the novel occurs when she travels to Howards End for the purpose of convincing Helen to break off her engagement to Paul Wilcox.

Helen Schlegel

The charming sister of Margaret, Helen is high-spirited and hopelessly idealistic. Beethoven's Fifth Symphony affects her most profoundly, and reveals an interesting theme in the novel. She hears a "goblin footfall" in the music, which she imagines to represent the "panic and emptiness" of life, but she also hears a repetitive motif that she imagines as the heroism, magnificence, and triumph of life. These two aspects of life intrinsically bound together echo the highs and lows of Helen's own experiences. Her short-lived love affair with Paul at the beginning of the novel is indicative of her behavior throughout—heady excitement followed by disillusionment. Ruled by passion, she seldom considers the reality of a situation until it is too late.

At first she is quite taken with all of the Wilcoxes, but the ill-fated love affair with Paul colors her feelings afterwards, and she is disappointed when Margaret and Henry Wilcox announce their engagement. Her liaison with Leonard Bast is the result of her sympathy for him and her anger at Henry, who will not help Leonard. Her anger at Henry also occasions a break with Margaret. Helen eventually reconciles with Margaret and Henry, who accept her and her illegitimate child (from Leonard Bast) at Howards End.

Margaret Schlegel

Margaret is the cultured, intelligent, and sympathetic protagonist of the novel. Although idealistic like her sister Helen, she is also very sensible and realistic. "Not beautiful, not supremely brilliant, but filled with something that took the place of both qualities—something best described as a profound vivacity, a continual and sincere response to all that she encountered in her path through life" is Forster's description of her. Some critics have found it hard to believe that Margaret would marry Henry Wilcox, a man most definitely her opposite. But Margaret sees things "whole," and although aware of Henry's faults, she also recognizes noble qualities in him. By the end of the novel, Margaret has had some effect on him. While it could be said that Helen reaches out to help Leonard, Margaret does the same for Henry. Indeed, Margaret is the connecting force between the Schlegels and the Wilcoxes; by the end of the novel,

Henry seems less "muddled" and Helen seems less impulsive. But this does not occur until after Margaret nearly leaves Henry because of his refusal to allow Helen to stay the night at Howards End with her. In her famous speech to him, she implores him to connect his infidelity with Helen's transgression: "You shall see the connection if it kills you, Henry! You have had a mistress—I forgave you. My sister has a lover—you drive her from the house. Do you see the connection? Stupid, hypocritical, cruel—oh, contemptible!—a man who insults his wife when she's alive and cants with her memory when she's dead. A man who ruins a woman for his pleasure, and casts her off to ruin other men. And gives bad financial advice, and then says he is not responsible. These, man, are you. You cannot recognize them, because you cannot connect."

Tibby Schlegel

Tibby is Margaret and Helen's younger brother, the Oxford undergraduate. Although intellectual like his sisters, he is not interested in personal relationships as they are. His placid demeanor plays comically against their more passionate personalities, and is particularly evident in the scene where Helen visits him at Oxford to let him know of her plans to go to Germany.

Charles Wilcox

Charles is the philistine elder son of Henry

Wilcox. Not especially fond of the Schlegels and their "artistic beastliness," he ridiculously suspects Margaret of scheming to get Howards End. His fierce sense of class superiority leads him to beat Leonard when he finds out that he is the father of Helen's child. Charles is convicted of manslaughter for Leonard's death.

Dolly Fussel Wilcox

Dolly is the chattering, good-hearted wife of Charles Wilcox. Like her husband, she foolishly believes Margaret is scheming to get Howards End.

Evie Wilcox

Evie, the daughter of Henry Wilcox, is a rather silly, superficial woman. Although she dislikes Margaret, she humors her father's interest in Margaret.

Media Adaptations

- *Howards End* was adapted for the stage by Lance Sieveking and Richard Cottrell and was produced in London in 1967.

- The BBC production *of Howards End*, adapted by Pauline Macaulay, was broadcast in 1970.

- A film adaptation of *Howards End* was released by Merchant Ivory Production in 1992, starring Emma Thompson and Anthony Hopkins. The film garnered nine Academy Award nominations, winning for Best Actress (for Thompson), Best Screenplay Adaptation, and Best Art Direction. It is available from Columbia TriStar Home Video.

Henry Wilcox

Henry is the head of the Wilcox clan, who marries Margaret Schlegel after the death of his wife, Ruth. Critic Rose Macaulay describes him this way: "He has the business mind; he is efficient, competent, unimaginative, practically clear-headed, intellectually and spiritually muddled, uncivilized, a manly man, with firm theories about women, politics, the Empire, the social fabric." He is not given to self-introspection, a trait that almost costs him his marriage to Margaret. She insists that he acknowledge the connection between his affair with Jacky Bast and Helen's involvement with Leonard Bast. But his flaw is that he lacks the ability to connect his actions with the pain they might cause in another person's life, thus his indifference to Leonard's loss of employment. Furthermore, he cannot relate his own transgressions in life to another person's similar transgressions; therefore, he cannot sympathize with Helen. He cannot "connect the prose with the passion." By the end of the novel, Henry is broken by the imprisonment of his son, Charles, which forces him to reevaluate his life.

Paul Wilcox

Paul is the younger Wilcox son with whom Helen briefly falls in love. The incident sets the tone for conflict between the Wilcoxes and the Schlegels.

Ruth Wilcox

Henry's first wife, Ruth, is a kind, unselfish woman whose family adores her. However, she completely mystifies her family after she bequeaths Howards End to Margaret. She does so because she intuitively senses that Margaret will appreciate its "personality" and significance. The critic Lionel Trilling has written that Howards End represents England and its agrarian past, and that Ruth, while not intellectual, possesses ancestral wisdom that will be passed on to Margaret. Ruth is almost like a spiritual guide, or as critic Rose Macaulay states, a bridge between the unseen and the seen, and Margaret believes herself and the others "are only fragments of that woman's mind."

Themes

Connection

The major theme of *Howards End* is connection—connection between the private and the public life, connection between individuals—and how difficult it is to create and sustain these connections. *Howards End* focuses mainly on two families: the Schlegels, who represent intellectualism, imagination, and idealism—the inner life of the mind—and the Wilcoxes, who represent English practicality, expansionism, commercialism, and the external world of business and politics. For the Schlegels, personal relationships precede public ones and the individual is more important than any organization. For the Wilcoxes, the reverse is true; social formalities and the rules of the business world reign supreme.

Through the marriage of Margaret Schlegel and Henry Wilcox, these two very different worlds are connected. Margaret, unlike her wildly idealistic sister Helen, moves toward an understanding of the Wilcoxes. Helen's initial encounter with the Wilcoxes proves disastrous, but Margaret begins to realize that many of the things she values, such as art and culture, would not exist without the economic and social stability created by people such as the Wilcoxes. "More and more," she says, "do I refuse to draw my income and sneer at those who guarantee it."

Margaret and Henry's marriage nearly comes to an end, however, when Henry is unable to make an important connection between his sexual transgression with Jacky Bast and Helen's liaison with Leonard Bast. Margaret and Helen want to spend the night together at Howards End before Helen returns to Germany to have her baby. But the hypocritical Henry cannot tolerate the presence of a "fallen woman" on his property, and refuses to allow Margaret and Helen to remain there for the night. As the critic Malcolm Bradbury has written, Margaret insists on the "primacy of the standard of personal sympathy" while Henry emphasizes "the standard of social propriety." Margaret and Helen defy Henry by staying the night at Howards End, where they reestablish their relationship. By the novel's end, events force Henry to reconsider his values. He is reconciled to Helen, and along with Margaret and Helen's illegitimate son, they live together at Howards End under Margaret's guardianship.

Class Conflict

Another important theme in *Howards End* concerns struggle and conflict within the middle class. The aristocracy and the very poor do not make an appearance in this novel; the novelist states that "[w]e are not concerned with the very poor," but instead with the "gentlefolk, or with those who are obliged to pretend that they are gentlefolk." The three families in *Howards End* each represent different levels of the middle class. The Schlegels occupy the middle position, somewhere between the Basts, who exist at the lower fringes of the middle class, and the Wilcoxes, who belong to the upper-middle class. Leonard Bast, the clerk, lives near the "abyss" of poverty, while the Schlegels live comfortably on family money, and Henry Wilcox, the wealthy business man who grows steadily richer, has money for "motors" and country houses.

Leonard Bast is somewhat obsessed by class differences, and tries to improve himself by becoming "cultured." He reads books such as Ruskin's *Stones of Venice* and attends concerts. He meets the Schlegel sisters at a concert performance of Beethoven's Fifth Symphony, and becomes interested in them mainly because they seem to take his intellectual aspirations seriously. The Schlegels are fascinated by Leonard and his situation, but Leonard's connection to the Schlegels ultimately proves fatal. When Margaret and Helen hear from Mr. Wilcox that the company Leonard works for is about to go bankrupt, they advise him to find another position. The information proves to be unsound, but Leonard follows it, taking and then losing another position. As a result, he and his wife Jacky are left nearly penniless. In the scene where Leonard, Jacky, and Helen storm into Evie's opulent wedding, Forster illustrates the huge social and economic gulf between the nearly destitute Basts and the wealthy Wilcoxes. This scene, as the critic Frederick P. W. McDowell has noted, "suggests that the impersonal forces by which the Wilcoxes prosper have operated at the expense of Leonard and his class."

Leonard is destroyed by a combination of the Wilcox's indifference and Helen's sympathy. Helen tries to convince Henry that he has a responsibility to help Leonard, because his advice essentially caused Leonard's ruin. When that proves futile, Helen's sympathy for Leonard overwhelms her and she sleeps with him. Upon discovering that Leonard is Helen's "lover," the brutish Charles Wilcox beats Leonard with the flat of the Schlegel family sword. Leonard dies not from the beating, but from a weak heart. He sinks to the floor, knocks over a bookcase and is buried in an avalanche of books, seemingly a victim of his own desire for self-improvement.

Future of England

Closely related to the themes of connection and class conflict in *Howards End* is the theme of inheritance. The novel concerns itself with the question of who shall inherit England. At the time *Howards End* was published, England was undergoing great social change. The issue of women's emancipation, commercial and imperial expansion, and the possibility of war with Germany were all factors that contributed to a general feeling of uncertainty about the future of England.

According to the critic Lionel Trilling, Howards End itself symbolizes England. It belongs to Ruth Wilcox, who descends from the yeoman class, and represents England's past. Before Ruth dies, she befriends Margaret Schlegel, and on her deathbed she scribbles a note leaving Howards End to Margaret. She cannot leave it to her family because the only feeling they have for it is one of ownership; they do not understand its spiritual importance as she knows Margaret will. The Wilcoxes dismiss Ruth's note as impossible, and disregard it completely, ignoring the rightful heir. But Margaret's connection with Ruth Wilcox in the novel is strong. Not only is she Ruth's spiritual heir, but she actually becomes Mrs. Wilcox and, ironically, inherits Howards End through her marriage to Henry.

Foster's answer to the question of who shall inherit England seems to suggest a shared inheritance. As the novel draws to a close, the intellectual Schlegels and the practical Wilcoxes are residing together at Howards End, and its immediate heir, Helen's illegitimate son, seems to symbolize a classless future.

Topics for Further Study

- Research the career of the famous German composer, Ludwig van Beethoven, focusing especially on his composition of the Fifth Symphony.

- Trace the evolution of the British Empire from 1910 to the Commonwealth of Nations today. What are some key differences between imperialist Britain of the Victorian and Edwardian eras and Britain now?

- What were the forces that led to WWI, and what was Britain's involvement?

- Analyze the history of the class structure in Britain. What were some of the political, social, and economic issues facing the proletariat class and the middle class in 1910? Can you relate them to Forster's depiction of Leonard and Jacky Bast?

Style

Setting

The various locales represented in *Howards End* are related to the theme of inheritance and which of England's landscapes—countryside, city, or suburbs—will claim the future. During the Edwardian era, a great migration from the countryside to the city transpired, mainly because England was shifting from an agrarian nation to an industrialized nation. London, in particular, was growing at an alarming rate, and a great deal of rebuilding and restructuring of the city occurred. New modes of transportation, such as the automobile, tramcars, autobuses, and the subway, allowed people more mobility than ever before. Urban and suburban development, or "sprawl," followed the subway and tramway lines. The novel is wary of this type of progress and movement, preferring the stability of the country life and homes like Howards End versus the impersonal, chaotic world of London.

The three families in *Howards End* occupy three different locales: the Schlegels live in London, the Wilcoxes split their time between homes in London and the countryside (easily facilitated by their "motor"), and the Basts live in suburbia. A great deal of movement occurs between country and city, and moving house is a major activity in the novel. For Ruth Wilcox, nothing is worse than being separated from your home. When she hears that the Schlegels' lease on Wickham Place will expire and they will be forced to move, she is greatly distressed. "To be parted from your house, your father's house—it oughtn't to be allowed…. Can what they call civilization be right, if people mayn't die in the room where they were born?" she says to Margaret.

Symbolism

Howards End is a highly symbolic novel; many critics have described it as parable with archetypal or mythic characters. The Wilcoxes symbolize the practical, materialistic, enterprising sort of people who have contributed to England's prosperity and strengthened the empire. The Schlegels symbolize the intellectual and artistic types who possess humanistic values and recognize the importance of the spirit. Margaret and Henry's marriage demonstrates the relationship between these two personalities, emphasizing a balance between the two.

Of all the Wilcoxes, Ruth is the only one who does not fit the Wilcox "mold." She is withdrawn from modern life, intuitive, spiritual, and not at all intellectual, but as Lionel Trilling states, representative of traditional values and ancestral knowledge. Along with Miss Avery, the caretaker of Howards End, Ruth Wilcox symbolizes the importance of the human connection to nature and the earth. The wych elm tree with the pig's teeth, the vine, and the hayfield at Howards End also emphasize this connection. The movement of the seasons and the rhythms of nature are contrasted to the senseless movement of the modern, industrialized city, symbolized by the motorcar. The motorcar is never portrayed in a very attractive light: chaos and confusion seem to follow it everywhere, as in the scene where Charles hits the cat.

Other important symbols include the Schlegel books and bookcase and family sword at Howards End, which play so significantly in Leonard's death. When Leonard falls from Charles's blow with the sword and literally buries himself in books, it appears that the culture and intellectual sophistication he so desperately sought become his ruin. It is noteworthy that the sword and books belong to the Schlegels, however. Ostensibly, it seems that Leonard dies at the hand of the Wilcoxes —Henry, by giving him bad advice, and Charles, by actually dealing the final blow with the sword. But if Helen had not been overwhelmed by her sense of injustice, her anger toward the Wilcoxes, and her pity for Leonard, he would at least still have his life. The novel's bitter irony is that the person who tried to help Leonard the most effectively destroyed him.

Humor

Forster received high praise for his use of humor. Many situations in the novel are quite satirical or ironic. One of the earliest comic scenes in the novel involves Aunt Juley's trip to Howards End on Helen's behalf. When Aunt Juley mistakes Charles for Paul, the comedy begins. The discovery of the error only leads to an argument over Helen's behavior, which progresses to an argument over which family is better, the Schlegels or the Wilcoxes. The silly argument betrays the well-mannered facade of two supposedly well-bred gentlefolk. It also foreshadows the more serious conflict that will arise between the two families.

Another humorous scene involves Margaret trying to engage Tibby in a discussion about his future. She wants Tibby to think seriously of taking up a profession after he graduates. Of course, her reasons have nothing to do with the need for money. Rather, she believes it would build character. When she mentions a man's desire to work, Tibby replies, "I have no experience of this profound desire to which you allude." The aesthetic Tibby has no reason to consider a profession because he is financially secure. One of his satirical comments is that he prefers "civilization without activity."

Another semi-comic scene is the Wilcox family meeting concerning Ruth's bequest of Howards End. The Wilcoxes operate the meeting in an impersonal, business-like manner that reflects their style. Their mistrust of personal relations leads Charles to suggest that perhaps Margaret manipulated his mother into leaving her Howards End. Dolly irrationally fears that Margaret, as they speak, may be on her way to turn them all out of the house. The scene illustrates how suspicious and ill-mannered the Wilcoxes can be, and how they always suppose people are trying to get something out of them.

Historical Context

The Influence of King Edward VII

The Edwardian Era is so named after King Edward VII of England. Although King Edward's reign spanned only nine years, from 1901–1910, many historians extend the period to the start of the First World War in 1914. King Edward's personality had a major influence on the attitude of the day; his hedonism characterized the era. He loved ceremonial and state occasions and enjoyed extravagant entertaining; in fact, one of his first undertakings as king was to redecorate the Royal Palaces. An avid sportsman, King Edward particularly enjoyed horse racing, hunting, and "motoring." Motoring, essentially viewed as a sport in the early years of Edward's reign, quickly became an indispensable part of everyday life. In *Howards End*, the Wilcoxes rely quite heavily on their motor.

The king surrounded himself with wealthy people, befriending those who had made their fortunes in new ventures like the railway and steamship industry, and the South African diamond mines. They conducted themselves in a crude, ostentatious manner, which the king enthusiastically embraced. King Edward was also a notorious womanizer, and his wife, Queen Alexandra, eventually resigned herself to his numerous affairs. Such behavior did not endear him to the old nobility, and inevitably King Edward's rakish ways came to symbolize a certain reaction against the primness of Victorian sensibilities. The pursuit of pleasurable diversions were the hallmark of the period, with outings to musical halls, theaters, sporting events and weekend parties in the country considered fashionable. In *Howards End*, Evie's weekend wedding at Onitron represents the Edwardian flair for lavish entertaining.

Despite his flamboyant social life, King Edward took an active part in important political issues. Well-traveled and fluent in several languages, the king participated in international affairs and helped establish better relations with France. The alliance with France became crucial as England felt increasingly challenged by the German economy in world markets. The threat of German dominance in Europe seemed real as Germany built up its navy and formed alliances with Austria-Hungary and Italy. The battle lines were being drawn for World War I, and an uneasy atmosphere pervaded all of Europe.

On the domestic front, one issue that captured the king's attention was the acute, widespread poverty in England. High unemployment plagued the urban areas, and welfare did not yet exist. Only a relatively small percentage of the population could live the opulent, glamorous lifestyle made fashionable by the king and his friends. The gap between the rich and the poor grew rapidly during this time; the rich were getting richer by investing in various moneymaking schemes in overseas markets throughout the Empire. Many people were troubled by the fact that poverty should be so common during a time of unprecedented prosperity. King Edward drew public attention to the issue by personally visiting some of the worst slums in London and reporting his experience to the House of Lords. He became a dedicated member of the Royal Commissions, whose task it was to alleviate the problems of the poor, and he supported the idea of state aid for the aged poor, which later became one of the first forms of welfare.

Social Change during the Edwardian Era

The Edwardian Era was a time of great social and political change. Industrialization, which had begun in the nineteenth century, forced many people to leave their farms for employment in the cities. By 1910, the majority of the population lived in urban areas. London, particularly, was expanding rapidly, and urban sprawl became a problem. The new tramway system and "tube train," which partly alleviated traffic congestion in downtown London, facilitated the growth of suburbia. A dramatic restructuring of downtown London occurred to accommodate more people and more new businesses, and many old buildings were torn down in the process. When the Schlegels' lease expires on Wickham Place, Margaret tells Ruth Wilcox that she supposes Wickham Place will be torn down and a new apartment building will be built in its place.

At the same time, many new inventions, such as the telephone, typewriter, electric motor, and the automobile, revolutionized daily life. Labor-saving devices such as the gas cooker and the vacuum cleaner allowed more time for leisure activities. In the growing business economy, the typewriter and the telephone were great assets, and opportunities for office workers grew. Many women filled these jobs, happy to leave the labor-intensive, low-paying jobs in the garment industry. Even well-to-do women began to pursue work outside the home. No longer content with only their embroidery or painting lessons, many wealthy women began opening their own businesses.

A dominant issue during the Edwardian Era was the issue of women's suffrage, and many women became involved in the movement. Early on, the suffrage campaign split into two factions, one group more militant than the other in its methods. The militant group, led by Emmeline Pankhurst and her daughters, employed tactics designed to attract widespread attention to the cause. Known as the "suffragettes," they began by heckling political meetings, breaking windows, and chaining themselves to railings. After 1911, however, women still had not received the vote, so the suffragettes initiated more violent strategies. The nation was shocked when they resorted to committing arson, cutting telephone wires, slashing paintings in public galleries, and throwing bombs. Imprisoned suffragettes held hunger strikes, which led to forcible feedings, which in turn led to fierce public debate. Finally, in 1918, women over 30 were given the right vote; women 21 and over were finally extended the same right in 1928. In *Howards End*, the Schlegel sisters are keenly interested in the suffrage issue and believe in equality for women, while the Wilcoxes dismiss the idea of women voting as pure nonsense.

Compare & Contrast

- **1910:** The British Empire includes India, Australia, New Zealand, Canada, Ireland, parts of Africa and Indonesia, and many islands scattered across the globe.
  Today: Many countries formerly a part of the British Empire have achieved sovereignty but hold membership in the Commonwealth of Nations, an association of independent and dependent nations which recognize the United Kingdom of Great Britain as Head of the Commonwealth.

- **1910:** The cost of a Rolls Royce is approximately 1,100 British pounds; less expensive motorcars can be had for approximately 200 British pounds.
  Today: The cost of a Rolls Royce is approximately 125,000 British pounds; less expensive cars can be had for approximately 6,000 British

pounds.

- **1910:** A college education at Oxford or Cambridge University is reserved only for the wealthy.
  Today: Scholarships and aid from state funds have made an Oxford or Cambridge education much more affordable.

- **1910:** For the first time in British history, a majority of the population lives in urban areas.
  Today: Approximately 80 percent of the British population lives in urban areas.

Critical Overview

Howards End was critically very well received in England upon its publication in 1910. Critics declared it the best of Forster's novels, with some proclaiming it Forster's masterpiece. An unsigned review in *The Times Literary Review* stated that Forster's "highly original talent" had found "full and ripe expression" with *Howards End*. Forster had begun to emerge as one of the greatest English novelists of his day.

In general, reviewers praised Forster's highly detailed and accurate portrayal of Edwardian society in the novel. "In subtle, incisive analysis of class distinctions, manners, and conventions, he is simply inimitable," proclaimed the *Morning Leader* in an unsigned review of *Howards End*. Forster also gained recognition for his creation of believable, compelling characters; his considerable powers of perception and imagination, especially concerning the complexity of human nature and relationships; and his keen wit and sense of humor, which he employed to great effect in his sometimes satirical depiction of England's upper classes. His poetical style and beautiful descriptions were singled out for praise, also. *The Times Literary Review* noted the "odd charming vein of poetry which slips delicately in and out of his story, showing itself for a moment in the description of a place or a person, and vanishing the instant it has said enough to suggest something rare and romantic and intangible about the person or the place."

Although the majority of reviews were extremely favorable, some critics felt certain aspects of plot development in *Howards End* seemed unrealistic. General criticism was expressed over whether Margaret would actually marry Henry, or whether Helen, a cultured Edwardian lady, would submit to a sexual encounter with a lower-middle class man like Leonard Bast. Others cited the sequence of events beginning with the highly coincidental death of Leonard, the resulting imprisonment of Charles, and Henry's subsequent "breakdown" as too convenient. Many reviewers found the resolution of the story somewhat artificial, "not representative," but "rather melodramatic." They questioned whether the Wilcox and Schlegel families could indeed come together at Howards End and live happily ever after. But even critics who found these plot developments implausible still endorsed the novel as a whole, with some admitting they were nitpicking at an otherwise great work.

Howards End remains one of Forster's most important novels, along with *A Passage to India*. Even though Forster published no more novels after *A Passage to India*, his popularity grew steadily in England and expanded to America with the publication of Lionel Trilling's book of criticism, *E.M. Forster*. Forster's novels, established early as classics, concern themselves with the mythic and archetypal aspects of human experience and all its complexities. His formidable talents as a writer include his realistic, yet ironical and satirical portraits of Edwardian society, a talent that aligns him with such great novelists as Jane Austen, and marks his novels as descendants of the English "novel of manners." Forster's novels are distinguished by their intense personal quality, their poetical style, their humor, insight, and intelligence as well as their committed humanism. Frederick P.W. McDowell has written that readers are attracted to Forster's works because of "a fascination exerted by characters who grip our minds; a wit and beauty present in an always limpid style; a passionate involvement with life in all its variety; a view of existence alive to its comic incongruities and to its tragic implications; and a steady adherence to humanistic values."

Film adaptations of Forster's work, including the Merchant Ivory production of *Howards End*, have widened Forster's audience. The posthumous publication of his letters, two short story collections, and a novel, *Maurice*, has continued his legacy. Widely considered a literary genius, Forster's works place him in the company of other great modern writers such as Virginia Woolf, Ford Madox Ford, Joseph Conrad, and D. H. Lawrence.

What Do I Read Next?

- In *Bloomsbury Recalled* (1996), Quentin Bell, son of Clive and Vanessa Bell, offers one of the most recent memoirs recounting the personalities and adventures of that famous literary group.

- Joseph Conrad's 1899 novel, *Heart of Darkness*, reveals the injustices of British imperialism in Africa.

- In Forster's first novel, *Where Angels Fear To Tread*, (1905) he contrasts the vibrant, free life of Italians with the artificial, hypocritical and bourgeois life of the suburban Londoners who visit an Italian village.

- Forster's novel, *The Longest Journey*, published in 1907 tells the story of two half brothers, one of them illegitimate.

- *A Room with a View* is Forster's 1908 novel about a young woman's love affair and her struggle with Victorian conventions.

- Forster's last and most highly regarded novel, *A Passage to India* (1924) details the social and historical milieu of colonial India, and one Englishwoman's experience there.

- Forster's posthumously published novel, *Maurice* (1971) tells the story of a young man's dis covery of his own homosexuality.

- Fellow Bloomsbury Group member Lytton Strachey revolutionized the genre of biography with his *Eminent Victorians*, offering unusually unflattering portraits of four British cultural heroes, including Florence Nightingale. Critics suggest that his incisive criticisms take on the difference between mere "moral righteousness" and "true humanitarianism."

- Virginia Woolf's 1925 novel, *Mrs. Dalloway*, is at once the story of Clarissa Dalloway's party and a critique of the British social system.

- Woolf's 1927 novel, *To the Lighthouse* focuses on the inner life and experiences of an English family.

Sources

Born, Daniel, "Private Gardens, Public Swamps: *Howards End* and the Revaluation of Liberal Guilt," *Novel: A Forum on Fiction*, Vol. 25, No. 2, 1992, pp. 141-159.

Bradbury, Malcolm, "Howards End," in *Forster: A Collection of Critical Essays*, edited by Malcolm Bradbury, Prentice-Hall Inc., 1966, pp. 131.

Crews, Frederick, *E.M. Forster: The Perils of Humanism*, Princeton University Press, 1962.

Levenson, Michael, "Liberalism and Symbolism in *Howards End*," in his *Modernism and the Fate of Individuality*, Cambridge University Press, 1990, pp. 78-93.

McDowell, Frederick P. W., "'Glimpses of the Diviner Wheels': Howards End," in *E. M. Forster*, revised edition, Twayne Publishing, 1982, pp. 82.

——————————, "'Unexplained Riches and Unused Methods of Release': Nonfictional Prose and General Estimate," in *E. M. Forster*, revised edition, Twayne Publishing, 1982, pp. 149-159.

Meisel, Perry, "Howards End: Private Worlds and Public Languages," in his *The Myth of the Modern: A Study in British Literature and Criticism after 1850*, Yale University Press, 1987, pp. 173-182.

Morning Leader, *"The part and the whole,"* October 28, 1910, pp. 3.

Review, in *The Times Literary Supplement*, No. 459, October 27, 1910, pp. 421.

Stone, Wilfred, "Howards End: Red-Bloods and Mollycoddles," in his *The Cave and the Mountain: A Study of E.M. Forster*, Stanford University Press, 1966.

For Further Study

Forster, E. M., *Aspects of the Novel*, E. Arnold, 1963.

> A collection of lectures delivered by Forster on the art of the novelist.

Forster, E.M., *Marianne Thornton: A Domestic Biography, 1797–1887*, Harcourt Brace, 1956.

> This biography of Forster's paternal aunt, Marianne Thornton, is also a study of Forster's own intellectual origins and family lineage.

Furbank, P. N., *E. M. Forster: A Life*, Harcourt Brace Jovanovich, 1978.

> The definitive biography of E. M. Forster.

Gardner, Philip, ed., *E.M. Forster: The Critical Heritage*, Routledge and Kegan Paul, 1973.

> This book is a collection of mostly early criticism on Forster's works.

Lago, Mary, and P.N. Furbank, eds., *Selected Letters of E.M. Forster*, 2 Vols., Belknap Press, 1983–1985.

> A collection of E. M. Forster's letters.

Lightning Source UK Ltd.
Milton Keynes UK
UKHW021846111019
351423UK00011B/936/P